WYNNS

The Last 20 Years

by

John Wynn

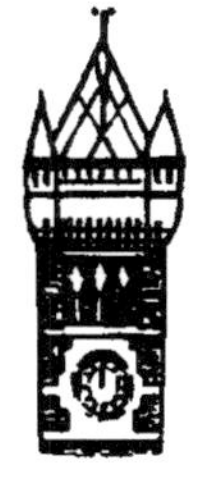

P.M. Heaton Publishing
Abergavenny, Gwent
Great Britain
1996

Front cover: Bill Wade driving Scammell Contractor HHB 361N (196) with a 170 ton rotor carried on a special rig between two straight girders on a pair of 6 line bogies, passes trailer No. 987 loaded with the 310 ton stator. At the time this GEC generator was the largest ever built in Britain and the eventual destination was the Enrico Fermi Nuclear Power Station in America. Mate Mike Hannen was sat in the passenger seat.

Title Page: Two of the three vessels transported from Birkenhead to the Shell Refinery at Stanlow.

Page 4: Scammell Contractor YAX 165T (631) was bought in 1979 and subsequently transferred within United Transport to Wrekin Roadways Ltd., of Telford.

Back cover: This 253 ton furnace was one of three delivered by WYNNS to Llanwern Steelworks. Transhipped to a pontoon from a vessel in the Bristol Channel, they were transported from the pontoon at a specially constructed berth – Porton Wharf, adjacent to the steelworks.

I dedicate this book to
my late wife Mo.

ISBN 1 872006 14 0

Published by P. M. Heaton Publishing
Abergavenny, Gwent, NP7 9UH

Printed in Great Britain by
The Amadeus Press Ltd.,
Huddersfield, West Yorkshire, HD2 1YJ

Typesetting by Highlight Type Bureau Ltd.,
Bradford, West Yorkshire, BD8 7BY

PREFACE

Thomas Wynn
1821-1878

It was with considerable pleasure that I saw how well my first volume – *WYNNS The First 100 Years* was received. It is clear from the many kind comments that I have had that WYNNS was a well regarded company and whilst it no longer exists it is far from forgotten. It had been my intention to compile this second volume, completing the history of the business. However, due to the wealth of material available I have confined this book to the last twenty years of operation in the United Kingdom alone, and will deal with the International side of the firm in a later book.

I would like to place on record my gratitude to all those who have helped with material, and hope that readers' enjoy this second volume as much as the first.

Sadly my wife *Mo* passed away during my work on this series. It was her determination and support that made all this possible.

John Wynn
Newport

October, 1996

Robert Wynn (1863-1923) his wife Nora, and family.
Children from left: George (O.G.), Emma, Hilda, Sam (the eldest), Percy (H.P.), Alan, R.T., and Gordon (the youngest).

N. Circ. Road A 406
Hatfield (A1)
Cambridge (A10)
The North
M1
WYNNS
For
5 miles
Motorway
M1
N. Circ. Rd. A406
Cambridge (A10)
Chelmsford (A12)
Brent Cross
Shopping Centre
Hendon Central
Finchley

WYNNS

WYNNS was founded in 1863 when Thomas Wynn, my great grandfather, realised the demand in South Wales for road transport and resigned from his job with The Great Western Railway to meet that demand. As the years passed the technology of road transport developed and so did WYNNS – from horses to steam traction engines to the internal combustion engine.

In 1923 the Company was incorporated under the title of Robert Wynn and Sons Limited thereby perpetuating the name of Thomas's son who had carried on the business after the death of its founder. Five of Robert's sons – Sam, R.T., George, Percy and Gordon – joined the business and under their leadership it was expanded throughout the thirties and early forties. During the period of nationalisation of the industry – 1947 to 1953 – WYNNS remained in family ownership and expansion was continued, to meet industrial development.

Although the company had depots at Newport, Cardiff, London and Welshpool (for timber extraction) after denationalisation WYNNS quickly expanded by opening a depot in Manchester to service heavy industry in the North of England, and some years later another depot was opened at Chasetown to offer an even better service to the industrial Midlands.

Expansion had brought its problems and by 1960 the five WYNNS brothers were asking themselves 'where do we go from here'? Financial advice was that a floatation on the stock market would be problematical. Firstly were WYNNS big enough? Secondly there had been years of a Conservative Government and there was a distinct possibility of a Labour Government with its policy of the re-nationalisation of road haulage. Thirdly it had to be accepted that the five brothers – and the driving force behind the success of the business – had passed or were approaching retirement age, leaving only R.T.'s son Noel and O.G.'s son John to continue in senior management with the name of Wynn.

The Wynns at the time of the sale of the business to United Transport.
From left: seated: R.T. and George. Standing: Noel, Percy, Gordon and John.

WYNNS – The new board of directors in 1964. From left seated: Percy Wynn, Duncan Foulds, R.T. Wynn, David Lloyd-Jones and Gordon Wynn. Standing: John Wynn, Noel Wynn, Bill Humphreys, Geoffrey Watts, George Wynn, Danny Williams and Jack Bown.

Thus they were advised against a stock market flotation and the only possibility of an injection of the capital required appeared to be the sale of the business. Pickfords made several approaches but the family were against this, bearing in mind the support WYNNS had had from its customers, and the certainty that the name would disappear.

In 1962 John Watts of Lydney, a friend of the Wynn's family and Chairman of United Transport, suggested that they talk to them. United Transport's subsidiary – Red & White Omnibus services had been nationalised under the 1947 Act and United had expanded into passenger transport operations in East and South Africa. The advice they had was that they had to secure investments in the United Kingdom to balance their overseas investments. Talks proceeded in a desultory manner. WYNNS were in no hurry as they were determined to celebrate the centenary of the business in 1963 still as an independent family concern, but towards the middle of that year agreement was reached on the basis that the sale was not to be completed until early 1964.

In November, 1963 WYNNS celebrated their centenary with a grand dinner in The Kings Head Hotel, Newport, and on the following Sunday they took over the streets of Newport with a parade of their vehicles – a horse and cart leading, followed by the Fowler traction engine DW 2121 towing the 1890 boiler wagon, and the rear brought up by their latest acquisition, a 48 wheeled 300 ton capacity trailer.

On February 7, 1964 the sale of the WYNNS business to United Transport was completed. David Lloyd-Jones became Chairman, R.T. became Deputy Chairman of the Company, whilst George took retirement but remained on the Board of directors; Percy and Gordon were appointed joint General Managers, Noel was promoted Deputy General Manager and remained as Company Secretary, with John on the Board, and Eddie Clark was elected to the Board.

During the 1960s, as well as much work in the U.K. with the Central Electricity Generating Board building Power Stations, the oil companies oil refineries, and many other industrial developments, WYNNS expanded into overseas markets.

As a private family concern WYNNS energies had to a large extent been channelled towards the development of large capacity trailers, but now as part of United Transport apart from continued expansion, large numbers of new motive units were acquired.

1964 had seen the sale of the timber extraction business and close of the Welshpool depot, and subsequently WYNNS withdrew from tippers with subsequent closure of the Cardiff premises.

The WYNNS concern was further strengthened in 1971 when the United Transport Company was sold to the British Electric Traction Co. Ltd. All went well for this period, but alas at the end of the seventies and the early eighties the bottom fell out of the heavy haulage market. The recession reduced the demand for electricity and oil – so that no more power stations or oil refineries were being built and with this no demand for the manufacture of the heavy equipment which would have been needed. Thus there was no demand for heavy haulage. Equally lack of finance overseas saw the ending of such developments in the third world.

WYNNS had to retrench and retrench quickly. The only manufacturer with anything like an order book was GEC at Stafford. Apart from WYNNS three depots at this time – Newport, Chasetown (Cannock) and

Left: WYNNS – Gordon (left), John and Percy at Newport in 1974.

Right: Some of the clerical and maintenance staff at the Newport Headquarters of WYNNS in 1974.

Manchester – United Transport had acquired Wrekin Roadways with its depot at Telford. Thus they had three depots within 50 miles of Stafford, and Newport was out on a limb. the painful decision was therefore made to close WYNNS headquarters at Newport as well as the depot at Chasetown, and to merge Wrekin Roadways and WYNNS with a new depot at Stafford to serve GEC. The amalgamated concern was thereafter known as WYNNS HEAVY HAULAGE. At this time the surviving members of the Wynn family still involved in the business – Noel and John – decided to withdraw, the former retiring and the latter resigning and thus neither moved to the new facility at Stafford.

As it turned out, this retrenchment did not help very much, as within a short period the WYNNS Manchester depot was closed and WYNNS were merged with the third heavy haulage company in the group, Sunter Brothers of Northallerton, to form a new company United Heavy Transport. Thus the well respected name of WYNNS had disappeared from the heavy haulage industry.

Again this arrangement only lasted for about a year. Econofreight, the Heavy Haulage arm of the Transport Development Group, had been having an equally difficult time, and another merger took place to form United Econofreight Heavy Haulage. Alas this only lasted until 1990 when the company was acquired by Brambles, the Australian forwarding and haulage group as part of their entry into the U.K. market.

Thus the once familiar name of WYNNS had long since disappeared from the roads of this country, but the memory of this old established haulage concern lives on in the hearts and minds of those who worked for or were associated with it. No individual could forget the sight of one of their heavy outfits proceeding slowly on its way. All would stop in admiration, never minding the delay – Oh what a sight.

WYNNS had been involved with the extraction of round timber since 1885, but with the acquisition of the firm by United Transport in 1964 they withdrew from this business.
One of the last jobs undertaken was at Itton Court, Chepstow. In the views *opposite above and overleaf* a pair of Caterpillar D6 Dozers are seen assisting a Douglas Timber Tractor in loading a Pole Trailer, and then winching the trailer to higher ground before coupling up for the road journey to the sawmill.

WYNNS

CARDIFF
223
WYNN'S

A Newport Corporation Leyland Double Decker bus is pictured being recovered from a reen near Duffryn High School, Newport in January, 1968. The ex-Military Lorain Mobile Crane, WDW 882 (Fleet No: 187) entered the fleet in 1961, and passed within the United Transport Group to Sunter Bros of Northallerton in 1968.

WYNNS operated a large fleet of mobile cranes mainly in the South Wales area.

WYNNS

WYNNS
SCAMMELL
WYNNS
BDW490C

A Scammell Highwayman low loader, BDW 490C (146) leaving the Isle of Wight Ferry after collecting a 17½ ton transformer from Shanklin for delivery to Maidenhead, in 1965.

The driver was Paddy Masterson, and with Stan Stuart and a further mate, was responsible for the loading and off-loading of this particular transformer themselves – a job they often undertook.

WYNNS added six of these units to the fleet during 1965.

WYNNS

This approach ramp for the Holyhead Car Ferry was transported on a Guy Invincible 8 wheeler XDW 300 (152) and steerable dolly combination from Fairfield-Mabey of Chepstow in 1965. It is shown on approach to and entering the Menai Bridge.

Due to the restricted columns on the Menai Bridge the load had to be tilted to an unusual angle determined by precise calculation. As is clearly shown below.

When moved in 1964 this English Electric transformer weighing 220 tons was the heaviest load moved in the United Kingdom by road. The load is shown en route from Stafford to the C.E.G.B. Power Station at Ferrybridge, Yorkshire. Three Pacific tractors were used with the 48 wheeled trailer 789.

The last Diamond T to enter the WYNNS fleet was this 1966 registered 929 type, EDW 782D (250) with a totally rebuilt cab. She is shown drawing a mobile stone crusher. In all a total of 22 Diamond T's were owned by the firm.

Three of four tanks 17ft 7ins in diameter by 11ft 11ins high were transported from London to Grangemouth Gas Works, Cardiff. The tanks had to be offloaded, slid under a bridge 12ft 8ins high and reloaded again by WYNNS before reaching their final destination. The three Guy Invincible 8 wheelers, dating from 1960/61 were XDW 300 (152), TDW 991 (294) and TDW 990 (293).

Two of WYNNS large fleet of tankers shown offloading into the tar tanker *Stella Maris* in 1965. Both Guy Warrier 8 wheelers, the vehicle facing was YDW 115 (156) dated from 1961. Shortly after this photograph was taken she was converted to a flatbed.

An 8 wheeled Guy Invincible, XDW 300 (152) laden with a deck unit manufactured by Fairfield Engineering Ltd., Chepstow for the construction of the George Street Bridge, Newport. WYNNS transported 32 of these sections each 56ft 10ins long by 12ft 9ins wide by 4ft 6ins high.

Another Guy 8 wheeler, TDW 991 (294) and dolly at the site of Newport's George Street Bridge, which was opened on 9th April, 1964.

One of four 132 ton auto transformers which were transported over the Weaver Navigational Canal. In order to accomplish this the bridge illustrated was specially assembled and subsequently dismantled by units of the Territorial Army. (1965).

A Guy 6x4 YDW 521 (101) with a specially lengthened low loader with well length of 53ft 4ins equipped with rear steering carries a V.C. 10 nose section from Preston Docks to the British Aircraft Corporation at Weybridge, Surrey, in 1965.

Overleaf Another view of the V.C. 10 nose section. Built by Short Bros., Belfast, it was one of ten nose and ten tail sections shipped from Belfast to Preston and then transported by road to Weybridge by WYNNS.

KEEP
LEFT

WYNN'S
BAR
GUY
INVINCIBLE

WYNNS
WYNNS
A. PRICE & Co LTD

During the construction of the Coldra Viaduct Section of the M4 Motorway near Newport in 1966 WYNNS were responsible for the transport of over 200 33-ton concrete beams which were each 100ft long. These were offloaded at railhead by WYNNS and conveyed to site and lifted into final position.

Opposite and above: A Scammell Highwayman, BDW 489C (145) and Guy Invincible, XDW 300 (152) are seen leaving the Mill Street Railway Sidings at Newport at the start of their journey to the Coldra. Note the steerable rear bogies being used, which originally were Diamond T Tractors.

Overleaf: The last of the beams to complete the project on arrival on site. Again 145 and 152 are shown, but many more units of the fleet were employed with the movement. The Author is shown (*right*) with Bernard James.

A tipper lorry is shown lying on the river bed following a road accident at Tredegar.

A WYNNS 25 ton mobile crane has arrived on the scene and has started to lift and recover the vehicle.

The lift has almost been completed, and the damaged lorry is soon removed. Note Gordon Wynn supervising.

Three WYNNS wreckers recovering a derailed railway wagon from a field near Ponthir in Gwent in September, 1969.
Above: The truck is righted. Two Ward le France and a modified AEC are used on the job.
Below: The railway wagon is towed through an underpass. The wrecker is an ex-MOD vehicle, fitted with a Gardner 6LW engine, and was rebuilt from an AEC Matador, finishing up with Scammell badging. Registered in 1966 as FDW 636D (215).

This Bedford KHA14 articulated unit, ADW 301B (125) was one of nine which WYNNS added to the fleet in 1964/65.

WYNNS were major operators of tipper lorries in the South Wales area. This Bedford KHTC14 eight tonner, BDW 383C (49) was one of fourteen acquired in 1964/65.

Model of the liner *Rotterdam*, the largest ships' model in the world, being exhibited outside the Civic Centre, Newport, before leaving to tour the country. The tractor unit was a Guy Invincible, TDW 288 (288). The Author is shown manoeuvering with the help of Bill Hayward. On the engine cover can be seen the Author's eldest son, Robert. John stresses it was impossible to avoid the kerb!

Two BCHC Iron Fairy Mobile Cranes, NDW 764G (269) and BDW 140B (270) being used to position equipment internally, at Messrs. Armco, Corporation Road, Newport, where there was restricted height clearance.

Some idea of the difficulties encountered in manoeuvering can be appreciated in these views of a Diamond T Drawbar tractor, BDW 277B (249) with a large vessel at Caerphilly.

This 98½ ton Pacific Class Locomotive and 34 ton tender *46235 City of Birmingham* is shown arriving and being offloaded at the Museum of Science and Industry at Birmingham in 1966. The Pacific drawbar tractor GDW 277 (192) was WYNNS first of this type which had entered service in 1951.

HAULAGE
R.H.A
ROAD HAULAGE
ASSOCIATION
WYNNS

Ready for the Commercial Motor Show at Earls Court, London in 1966, WYNNS first Scammell Contractor, FDW 769D (188) was the main exhibit on the Scammell Lorries Stand. She is shown resplendent in her newly applied WYNNS livery.

WYNNS post-war expansion in heavy haulage had been achieved by their development of large capacity trailers, and their innovative ideas in using pneumatic tyres and hydraulic suspension ahead of all others. Support for all this had been provided by the acquisition of ex-Military vehicles, comprising six Pacific and twenty-two Diamond T Drawbar tractors, which were all eventually re-engined, and re-cabbed by their own staff.

With the sale of the business to United Transport, whilst the development of other sides of their business continued, and large numbers of new vehicles were acquired, they set about renewing the heavy haulage tractor unit fleet. Much discussion took place with Scammell Lorries Ltd., of Watford, and they decided to purchase vehicles of the Contractor range tailored to their own requirements. In all the fourteen years from 1966 twenty five Scammell Contractors entered the fleet. Initially four 100 ton units were bought, but this was followed by six of 150 ton and fifteen of 240 tons.

As with the Pacifics' before them, the heaviest units, the fifteen of 240 tons capacity were all individually named, the selection being made by the author. The vehicles are all listed hereunder:

YEAR INTO FLEET	FLEET NO.	REGISTRATION.	NAME	TYPE
1966	188	FDW 769D	–	100
1966	189	GDW 231D	–	100
1966	190	GDW 249D	–	100
1967	186	GDW 848E	–	100
1967	185	JDW 147F	–	150
1967	183	JDW 247F	–	150
1969	182	NDW 836G	Conqueror	240
1969	184	NDW 837G	Challenger	240
1969	187	NDW 838H	Supreme	240
1969	191	NDW 839H	Crusader	240
1970	198	SDW 545J	–	150
1970	200	SDW 937J	–	150
1971	280	TDW 83J	–	150
1971	281	UDW 139J	–	150
1974	193	RDW 339M	Hercules	240
1974	194	SDW 173N	Champion	240
1974	195	GTX 211N	Resolute	240
1974	196	HHB 361N	Talisman	240
1976	600	KAX 395P	Renown	240
1977	602	RWO 73P	Superior	240
1077	604		Illustrious	240
1979	628	XAX 512T	Cavalier	240
1979	631	YAX 165T	Buccaneer	240
1979	633	YWO 24T	Musketeer	240
1980	640	DBO 661V	Invincible	240

Of these the 1979 Scammell 631 (YAX 165T – Buccaneer) after about a year in service with WYNNS was transferred within United Transport to Wrekin Roadways Ltd., of Telford, Shropshire, to become their fleet number 337.

In addition WYNNS pioneer Pacific from 1951, Dreadnought (192 - GDW 277) was completely rebuilt using Scammell parts in 1969, and re-appeared with her same name and fleet number, but re-registered as NDW 345G.

This was a formidable fleet of heavy tractors which helped enable WYNNS to maintain their position as a leader within the heavy haulage industry.

This Scammell 240 ton Drawbar tractor, NDW 837G (184) was one of four added to the fleet during 1969.

Ferranti
TRANSFORMER
Ferranti
TRANSFORMER
NEWPORT & MANCHESTER
WYNN'S
WYNNS
WYNNS
HEAVY HAULAGE
NEWPORT-LONDON
CONTRACTORS
MANCHESTER
WYNNS
WYNN'S
HEAVY HAULAGE
NEWPORT·MANCHESTER·LONDON
DREADNOUGHT
192
192
GDW 277

The first ever 400,000 volt transformer, weighing 212 tons, conveyed on trailer 789 with three Pacific Drawbar tractors, from Ferranti at Hollingwood to the Central Electricity Generating Board, at Monk Fryston, Yorkshire.
It should be remembered that at this time the heavy load route was via Huddersfield/Leeds, necessitating the long climb of Standedge over the Pennines which would have taken three hours, with the addition of a fourth tractor.

WYNNS
NEWPORT · MANCHESTER · LONDON
197
WYNNS
HEAVY HAULAGE
AEI
TRANSFORMER

AEI
TRANSFORMER
WYNN'S
CRANE
WYNN'S 451A
450A

These photographs show the first use being made of the Air Cushion equipment, which was specially developed by the CEGB in conjunction with British Hovercraft. This was designed to relieve excess axle weights on bridges. It is being used here with trailer 789 moving a transformer manufactured by AEI en route to Legacy in 1967. Note above Jack Grady, the Chief Transport Engineer for the CEGB with H.P. Wynn – both looking very serious.
On Monday, 31st January, 1977 WYNNS achieved the 1000th blow of bridges with this equipment.

Above: Tommy Cromwell can be seen signalling in his inimitable way. Heading a Ferranti transformer with his Pacific drawbar tractor, a further two are pushing at the rear, at the start of a journey to Eggborough.

Right: Steersman John Dickson shown concentrating on his job, on the delivery of the remaining two transformers into Frodsham.

WYNNS

THE HIXON DISASTER

On Saturday, 6th January, 1968, eleven people died when a Manchester to Euston Express Train sliced our trailer No. 654 in half whilst it was negotiating the automatic level crossing at Hixon loaded with a 120 ton transformer tank.

I believe that enough was said about this sad event at the time, in the press, and at the subsequent Public Enquiry, for me not to elaborate further.

However, one fact that was not highlighted in any way was the bravery of our back tractor driver Alan Illsley in staying at his post. He was driving a Diamond T tractor and consequently sitting on the nearside, the same side on which the train was approaching our vehicle. Instead of jumping he continued to push the load in an attempt to get it clear. Bearing in mind that this action was causing the Diamond T to get ever nearer the line on which the express was travelling, this was in my opinion, very brave.

I am only sorry that it has taken 28 years for it to be recognised in print.

Above: This Guy Invincible articulated flat 612 DW (96) is laden with 40ft pipes for the North Sea Gas Grid, manufactured at Stewart & Lloyd's Corporation Road Works, Newport. The vehicle is shown at the Old Green Crossing, Newport, with the Castle Hotel in the background.

Left: This Guy Invincible articulated tractor, DDW 482C (235) seen unloading Gas pipes, was part of a large number of Guy lorries in the fleet.

Below: Three tractor units engaged on container work – two Guy Big J tractors, NDW 188G (228) and RDW 625H (73) together with a Scammell Trunker 2 vehicle, KDW 206F (252).

100ft steel girders en route from Fairfield-Mabey of Chepstow is shown negotiating the streets of the town shortly after leaving the manufacturers yard, in charge of a Scammell Contractor, GDW 231D (189).
Top: The outfit turns into the main street.
Above: Negotiating to pass through the Arch, under the direction of Ern Adams.
Above right: Almost through the arch, giving some idea of the tight squeeze.
Below right: Passing from the town with a long climb still ahead. The eventual destination was the new British Rail Bridge at Begelly, near Tenby, West Wales.

WYNNS
SCAMMELL
CUMMINS
GDW
231D
WYNNS
SCAMMELL
CUMMINS
GDW
231D
WYNNS

Fortunately it was a very rare occurrence when a job didn't go smoothly, and consequently I will never forget the Butane Tanks to Stornoway.

I won a contract from John Thompson Horseley Bridge at Wolverhampton to transport two Butane Storage Tanks 85ft long x 12ft diameter and weighing approx. 30 tons from their works to the Isle of Lewis.

For the sea crossing from Port of Rhu, Glasgow to the island Thompsons arranged an Army Tank Landing Craft called *Akyab* to carry us over.

My first mistake was not having the Captain with me when I flew over to do the usual site inspection. This omission resulted in the LCT not coming ashore at the spot I had chosen as being ideal for us. The reason was that hidden rocks that I had not seen because of the state of the tide when I visited, prevented the Captain from making this approach.

The first part of the operation from Wolverhampton went well with Ron Bailey and Len Smith in charge of the two vessels. I picked Ern Adams up at 5am on a Saturday morning in July, 1969 and drove North where we met the outfits on the outskirts of Glasgow and managed to persuade the Police to escort us that afternoon rather than their preferred time of 8pm. The LCT was in position and we loaded Len's vessel with his Diamond T tractor, a 4 wheel Albion loaded with plates and timber and Ern's 4 wheel drive AEC tackle wagon.

I managed a good nights sleep and was very surprised when rising and going for breakfast to find that we had been in a Force 8 gale for most of the night.

Fortunately the rest of the trip was fairly calm and first thing on the Monday morning we approached the beach. This was when I realised we were making for a spot a long way from where I had planned. This due to the rocks mentioned earlier.

I shall always remember the large crowd of islanders who had turned out to witness what they thought was going to be a unique but expertly carried out landing operation.

Len Smith drove the Diamond T off the ramp and after turning left immediately became stuck. As the tide was still coming in I asked an islander how high up he thought the water would come. He put a finger halfway up the fuel tank and so it turned out to be.

We next discharged the Albion then the AEC who both managed to gain high hard ground. As these operations had taken longer than anticipated the Captain decided to move around to the town quay and resume again that afternoon when the tide was again coming in.

Ern had positioned the Diamond T and the AEC to power winch the vessel ashore and this operation commenced as soon as the LCT was in position. I was on the LCT and Ern was on the shore. What neither of us was aware of was that the power we were applying to move the load along the deck and towards the bow doors was tending to pull the LCT more onto the shore. To counter this the Captain ordered slow astern on his engines and thus balanced out the two forces. Due to the tight clearance between the bow door frames we were having difficulty in manoeuvering the load. In fact the tying on equipment became detached so that I stopped the job to retie the vessel onto the bogies. Ern was not impressed by this delay.

After some thirty minutes of effort we at last positioned the load to pass between the bow door frames and with that it started to exit quite quickly with the power of the shore winch. It was then that we realised that the LCT was now reversing off the shore as the engines were still in reverse, but were no longer counter balancing the pull ashore.

I will never forget the site of the back bogie disappearing off the end of the ramp into deep water and the consequent splash. Fortunately because of the retying on, the vessel stayed on the bogie. The watching islanders must have been very confused with this incident.

Due to the high tide we were unable to tackle the recovery until 11pm that day. We managed to move the outfit part way off the beach but the incoming tide prevented us from getting clear. We were able to engage the services of a JCB whose driver was fortunately a true professional. It still took us another day to clear the beach and then another half day to get to site and offload.

The second vessel was discharged from the LCT and onto site in less than one day, so we had obviously learnt from experience.

Above: Loading the first Butane Storage Tank onto the Army Tank Landing Craft *Akyab* at Port of Rhu, Glasgow.

Left and below: At sea in the LCT on passage to the Isle of Lewis.

First ashore – Diamond T 3630 DW soon became stuck.

The Albion Clydesdale 4 wheeler FDW 536D (164) was more fortunate as she reversed off the LCT.

The Butane Tank in the sea. Waiting for the tide to recede.

An impressive view of the stranded vessel.

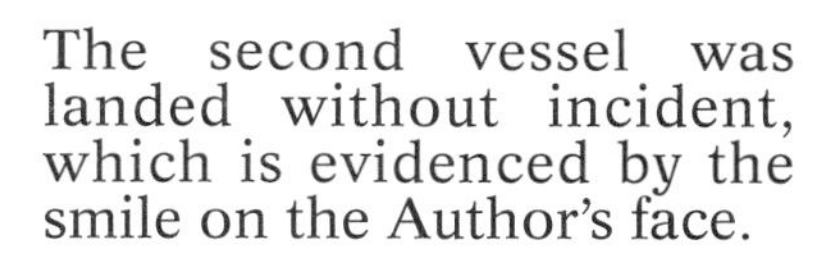

The second vessel was landed without incident, which is evidenced by the smile on the Author's face.

The job completed – the two Butane Storage Tanks offloaded in final position.

Vessel sections manufactured by Whessoe Ltd., Darlington were conveyed from Swansea Docks to the Lummus Company's site at B.P. Chemicals, Baglan Bay, Port Talbot and the National Oil Refinery at Llandarcy, in 1970. The vessels measurements varied from 32ft to 57ft long by 22ft 1 1/2 ins diameter and weighed up to 63 tons. In the front of this pair Scammell Contractor, NDW 837G is coupled to an eight in line bogie, whilst the rear vehicle is a six line bogie drawn by NDW 836G.

On Page 52 are two further views.

WYNNS
SCAMMELL
182
NDW
836G
WYNNS

WYNNS

WYNNS were able to offer throughout deliveries of heavy loads to the U.S.A. and Canada with the cooperation of Atlantic Container Lines and Lockwood Bros., of Virginia. The load did not leave the carrying platform from the time of collection to time of delivery.
Scammell, GDW 231D is seen loading such a load onto a ship at Liverpool Docks.

A 207 ton Stator negotiating the 1 in 6 Buttrills Hill, Barry, South Glamorgan, with the assistance of five tractor units (only four in view) in 1971. The Stator was collected from the A.E.I. works at Trafford Park, voyaged by roll-on/roll-off vessel from Manchester Docks to Barry, then delivered by WYNNS to Aberthaw Power Station. NOTE - Mrs. Elsie Anderson, wife of Chief Engineer Stan Anderson, can be seen standing in the re-built Pacific.

ROWE
HUMPHRY
DAVY
LICENSED
WYNNS
JDW
247F

The combined use of road, sea and “air” transport moved this 162 ton super-grid transformer from Hawker Siddeley’s works, Walthamstow, to the Central Electricity Generating Board’s Substation at Indian Queens, Cornwall in 1971. WYNNS conveyed the load throughout – first to Tilbury docks, thence by roll-on/roll-off vessel to Penzance when, after negotiating the main street of the town and the ‘S’ bend at the Western end of Market Jury Street (which many people thought impossible), air cushion equipment was fitted to the trailer to relieve bridges en route to its’ destination.

A 240 ton Scammell Contractor, NDW 836G (182) leads whilst a 150 ton model JDW 247F (193) pushes.

Two further views of this movement are shown overleaf.

PLY JOINT SOLE AGENTS
HARTNELL, TAYLOR & COOK.
O. THE MALL, CLIFTON, BRISTOL 8.
elephone: 39064/5.
TREGLOWN & SONS
CHAPEL STREET, PENZANCE, Cornwall
phone Penzance 3843/4.
ROYAL
WYNNS
WYNNS
HAWKER SIDDELEY POWER TRANSFORMERS
HAWKER SIDDELEY POWER TRANSFORMERS
SCAMMELL

WYNNS
WYNNS

HOLSCHER

An Aerial view of Porton Wharf in the Bristol Channel.

In 1973 three furnaces, 27ft in diameter by 28ft high weighing 253 tonnes were delivered by WYNNS to the British Steel Corporation, Spencer Works, Llanwern, Newport. They had been manufactured by Head Wrightson Process Engineering Ltd, and transported from the North East by the Holscher Line Heavy Lift Vessel *Gloria Siderum* and transhipped to a pontoon barge at Newport Deeps in the Bristol Channel. Porton Wharf – a specially constructed berth was engineered further up channel where WYNNS rolled on to the Pontoon, up-lifted the pieces by the trailer's own Hydraulic Suspension, rolled off and travelled by road to the delivery point within the steel plant. The trailers used had seven lines of axles with three axles on each line making the trailer 19ft wide, which provided a very advantageous stability factor. On each delivery the trunnion ring was also handled in a similar manner, these being 28ft in diameter x 13ft high and weighted 134 tons.

On the following two pages are illustrated the furnaces and trunnions being moved off the pontoon prior to transporting into the steel works.

The group depicted at the foot of page 61 shows the WYNNS gang who installed the furnaces in their final position. From the left: Bill Pitten, Vic Tremlett, Colin Parsons, Colin Kirby, Bernard James, Peter Collier, Peter Faulkner, Ken Johnson, Author, Ern Adams and Rex Evans.

HOLSCHER

HEAD WRIGHTSON
are engineering
HOLSCHER
WYNNS

HEAD WRIGHTSON
WYNNS

WYNNS
HEAD WRIGHTSON
SCAMMELL
CONQUEROR
NDW
836G

103/1
WYNNS
U.K.
WYNNS
U.K.

WYNNS
DREADNOUGHT
192
192
NDW 345G
WYNNS
HEAVY HAULAGE

HEAVY HAULAGE
WYNNS

LONG
VEHICLE

WYNNS tanker fleet expanded greatly to over twenty units in this period. From the original tar and sulphuric acid products, specialised tankers carried a variety of cargo including Maleic Anhydride, Polystyrene pellets, wax products, bitumen liquid pitch, anthrarcine and petroleum products throughout the country.

Pictured at the Newport works of Monsanto Chemicals Ltd are two 3,500 gallon tankers. These vehicles hired out by WYNNS on long term basis carried the customers own livery. The tractor units were a Scammell Handyman 3 – PDW 441H (175) dating from 1969 and a Seddon EDW 399D (170) from 1966 which was fitted with a Gardner 6LX engine.

This 1968 Scammell Trunker 2 tractor unit KDW 278F (253) is seen outside the Newport Headquarters of WYNNS coupled to a new stainless steel tank trailer.

This twin tipping powder tanker trailer is show with an ERF 'B' series, TDW 297S (620) dating from 1978.

This 1976 Seddon Atkinson tractor unit KAX 391P with tri-axle tank semi-trailer is pictured at Monsanto Chemicals, Newport. She carried the fleet number 243.

This pair of Guy Big J4 articulated tankers NDW 188G (228) and ODW 132G (67) dated from 1969. WYNNS distinctive livery is shown to good effect on the rear of the tankers.

A Guy 8 wheeler delivering a valve during the construction of Rhyader Dam. The lorry arrives on site, the valve is off-loaded and lowered to the floor of the dam. The flat bed follows, and the valve is reloaded, and then driven into position for off-loading and final positioning by WYNNS Heavy Gang.

Two six line bogies receiving a 140 ton vessel, 140ft long and 16ft in diameter from a Van der Laan ship beached in Galliwick Bay, Milford Haven. The first of two delivered to the Amoco Refinery in 1972. Scammell Contractor NDW 837G (184) has nosed the outfit into position.

A 370 ton 144ft by 18ft 4ins diameter platform reactor being delivered to Shellhaven, in 1974. The reactor had come from Italy on a Hansa ship and pontoon. WYNNS loaded it on the pontoon using the built in hydraulic equipment of the bogies. After rolling off it negotiated a 360 degree turn and then travelled the mile to the Shell Refinery.

Scammell NDW 836G (182) is in attendance. Out of sight is NDW 837G (184). Involved in these moves were drivers Bill Wade and Syd Davies with mates Bill Pocock, John Baulch and Mike Galliford. Subsequently later in that year WYNNS received a further two Japanese reactors at 385 tons each. The whole contract was carried out on behalf of John Mowlem.

Above: Approaching and *below* inside the access tunnel leading to the underground working face of the British section of the first Channel Tunnel in 1975 (which was subsequently abandoned). Shown is the cutting face of a 196 ton 17ft 3ins diameter boring shield loaded on a 7 axle bogie, after negotiating a 500 yard descent of 1 in 6.
Personnel on this job were drivers, Ken Preece and Roger Banfield with mates John Dickson, Bill Pocock and Albert Vincent. Eric Anderson from WYNNS maintenance staff was also involved.

Custom built for an American, the luxury motor yacht measured 114ft long, 24ft wide, 35ft high, weighing 100 tons, was carried to the Medway using a special ten line 19ft wide flat top-bogie. Scammell Contractor NDW 838H (187) is used.

This paper cyclinder, weighing 105 tons was transported by WYNNS from the makers Walmsleys Bury Ltd to Henry Cooke Ltd., at Beetham, Cumbria in 1974. WYNNS were responsible for jacking the cylinder up a height of 15ft before sliding it into final position in the Mill. Its arrival aroused considerable interest as shown.

A 230 tons Bessemer Converter Shell 35ft long by 28ft 6ins in diameter and a 245 ton trunnion ring, the first of two pairs loaded by WYNNS Heavy Gang from a Heavy Lift Ship at Port Talbot Docks and transported to the new B.O.S. plant at British Steel's Margam Works, in June, 1968.

An impressive view of the outfit with Pacific 196 – GDW 585 leading, appears overleaf. Bernard James is shown keeping a watching eye.

WYNNS

WYNNS
WYNNS
196
HEAVY HAULAGE
HEAVY
HAULAGE

WYNNS

Opposite: A transformer being loaded aboard the Blue Star Line heavy lift ship *Australia Star* for export, from a WYNNS outfit headed by NDW 836G (182).
Above: A vessel measuring 90ft long x 17ft diameter x 20ft over projections en route from Dudley to Liverpool Docks for shipment to Canada. Although the load was carried in end suspension to reduce travelling height it still created many routing and operating problems.
Left: These 100 ton Battleship gun barrels were transported from Shoeburyness to the Imperial War Museum, London, where WYNNS also mounted them on their permanent display. Without the intervention of the museum's curator these barrels, the last of their kind, would have been lost for ever. *Facing from the left:* Ern Adams, Vic Tremlett and Bill Kirkland.

The Auxiliary Ketch *Lusiada* measuring 60ft long by 17ft high and 17ft wide, weighing 60 tons was transported from Staffordshire to Liverpool.

Pictured in front of a 338 ton Parsons Peebles Transformer at Granton Dock are the Author and Wife Mo. This was the largest transformer built in Britain up to 1977 and was about to be taken on board ship for delivery to the North of Scotland's Hydro Electric Power Station at Peterhead.

A special 6 axle articulated outfit rolls along the access to the Pandoro Ferry at Fleetwood in 1979. Loaded with an 85 tonne engine manufactured by APE-Crossley Ltd., of Manchester, this was one of the heaviest RO/RO shipments ever moved through the port of Larne.

This 1980 Scammell Contractor Mk. 2 DBO 661V (640) heads a flat top bogie loaded with an Oxygen Box through London under Police escort.

Top: Scammell JDW 147F (185) operating as a low loader, laden with the locomotive *Foxcote Manor* en route to Oswestry, driven by Alan Peryer, assisted by John Hewlett and 'Nipper' Barry.

Centre: Atkinson 6x4 NDW 52M (97) with the tender for the above locomotive.

Bottom: 185 again, this time carrying a Saddle tank locomotive.

Atkinson 6x4 low loader, DDW 813L (96) seen passing the Coach and Horses Inn at Castleton, between Newport and Cardiff.

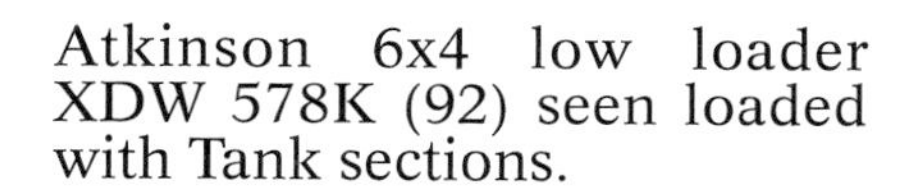

Atkinson 6x4 low loader XDW 578K (92) seen loaded with Tank sections.

A trio of Atkinson 6x4 tractor units – PDW 794M (232), DDW 813L (96) and EDW 480L (230).

Three of five Sand Filters 37 tonnes each and 12.192m x 3.962m x 4.267m high, en route from Danks of Netherton's Oldbury Works to Serck Water Processing at Gloucester and then later delivered to the new terminal at Sullom Voe. Three Atkinson 6x4 low loaders are being used led by HBO 753N (100).

A cased load is carried by Atkinson low loader, NDW 53M (98), and is shown leaving the premises at Albany Street.

Foden AUH 65T (635) is seen travelling in Newport Docks laden with a catamaran, 20ft wide in 1980. The famous Newport Transporter Bridge can be seen in the background.

A Volvo 6x4 step framed outfit AAX 542T (618) is seen with a tank, in 1980, en route to Shell Chemicals at Carrington.

A 108 ton pressure vessel 66ft long x 35ft wide x 14ft diameter being moved locally within the Proof and Experimental Establishment at Pendine in 1977. WYNNS were also responsible for the loading and off-loading operations and the move was over a distance of some 4 miles involving power line removals and road and site preparations due to the extreme width. Scammell Contractor HHB 361N (196) was used.

Scammell Contractor JDW 147F (1985) shown *above* operating as a drawbar tractor drawing a vessel and *below* as an articulated outfit laden with a crawler crane.

Above: JDW 147F back again operating as a drawbar tractor, heading a particularly wide load, a 20ft diameter paper drying cylinder from Walmsley of Bury.
Below: Pictured alongside Scammell XAX 512T (628) on Sunday, 8th October, 1978, *from left* Commander Brian Fairbairn in charge of escorts through the Metropolitan Police Area, the Author, and Jack Grady, the Chief Engineer for the CEGB. Trailer No. 987 is fitted with Series 2 Air Cushion Equipment and loaded with a 260 ton Stator from Kingsnorth Power Station to Littlebrook Power Station.

Scammell KAX 395P (600) with Nicholas Low Loader is shown with two different large diameter vessels.

2360 tons of Oxygen, Nitrogen
and Argon will be made from
Texas air every day with this
British built unit —
Made by
BOC-AIRCO
CRYOGENIC PLANT LIMITED
WYNNS
WYNNS

Top: A convoy of Centurion tanks is shown, all being carried on purpose built tank transporter trailers coupled to Diamond T drawbar tractors.

Opposite: An Air Separator Unit, one of five is shown being lifted off at the Royal Victoria Docks, London in 1970 prior to export to the U.S.A. after its' journey from BOC., Edmonton. Scammell NDW 837G (184) was driven by Billy Wade.

Above: A Dewaxing Filter Unit leaving the premises of Fletcher and Stewart Ltd., Derby, in the charge of SDW 937J (200).

TOP
R.H.
LIFEBUOY

This 32.46m x 2.44m diameter Boiler Drum weighing 251 tonnes, was one of three delivered by WYNNS to the C.E.G.B. Littlebrook "D" Power Station for N.E.I. John Thompson Ltd., Thompson Pressure Vessels Division, Wolverhampton. The movement involved both road and sea in its' delivery. (1976)

Above: Two further views of the Boiler Drum move. Driver Roger Banfield can be seen sprinting to catch up his tractor now driven by the Author. Also shown behind Roger is Tom Gregory, and at the rear can be seen steersman Ken Johnson.

Left: View taken by the Author's wife Mo from the bridge at Junction 13 on the M6 shows the outfit proceeding towards Stafford.

Four views of the installation of a 258 ton GEC inner stator at Heysham. During the road journey from Stafford to roll on the *Aberthaw Fisher* at Pomona Dock, Manchester, the C.E.G.B. air cushion relief system was used to cross seventeen bridges. On arrival at Heysham the trailer was manoeuvered into a very restricted area, off-loaded on to a special steel runway and winched sideways 60 feet. WYNNS then moved it endways 60 feet on to a special timber and steel support and with the use of their 400 ton capacity electric jacks lowered it 13 feet on to sole plates for its insertion into the outer cover as shown. Similar installations were carried out at Hinkley Point 'B' and Hartlepool Power Stations.

Left: The crew who were responsible for the installation *from left* Dave Minton, John Perola, Bernard James, Barry Setterfield, Gerry Gard, Pete Collier, the Author and Ern Adams.

Photographed at the Albany Street, Newport Headquarters of WYNNS – four Scammell Contractor Drawbar tractors YWO 24T (633) Musketeer, YAX 165T (631) Buccaneer, DBO 661V (640) Invincible and RWO 73R (602) Superior, are flanked by two Scammell Amazon 100 ton articulated units AHB 807T (632) and FBO 993V (636). The Author is standing in front with the Workshop foreman Eric Anderson and Cliff Atherton.

The main attraction at the 1976 Commercial Motor Show at Earls Court on the Leyland Special Vehicles Stand was this Scammell Contractor 240 ton tractor 602 – Superior which was to enter service as RWO 73R.

Scammell FDW 769E (188) driven by Gerry Gard has just stopped and allowed the traffic to pass on the approach to Raglan from Abergavenny on the A40. The Police Officer escorting was P.C. 427 Mike Curr, using a BSA 650cc Thunderbolt motor cycle, KAX 303D – which was the allocated machine of the publisher of this book – Paul Heaton.

JDW 147F (185) operating as a low loader shown carrying a tank for the army.

At the premises of Parsons Peebles at Whitton (formerly GEC) showing trailer 789 exiting the very confined loading bay with a 200 ton stator for Didcot Power Station. Note the use of steel plates on the opposite footpath.

The Author's youngest son Peter with Rex Evans in front of his Pacific YDW 356 (195) on Malpas Road, Newport.

Author's sons Robert *(left)* and Peter with Ivor Peake, Workshop foreman at Albany Street.

Peter Wynn *(Left)* , secretary Janet Erickson and Alan Peryer shown in front of a new Scammell Contractor, YWO 24T (633) Musketeer.

Apart from transporting the biggest loads, WYNNS were also responsible for carrying the prettiest of young ladies. Big supporters of Newport Carnival, supplying many of the floats, WYNNS always provided a new vehicle to transport the Carnival Queen and her attendants.

End suspension was a new method of carrying transformers which was developed by English Electric at Stafford. Six 230 ton transformers were conveyed by this method to Didcot Power Station and a further six to Pembroke Power Station.
Above: Two original middleweight Scammell Contractors 185 and 187 are shown transporting a transformer by this method in 1969.
Below: H.P. Wynn (*left*) is shown with Jim Webberley of English Electric who was responsible for the end suspension design.

Looking back on the Stanlow job it seems incredible that I never jumped on a plane and flew to Holland where the vessels were being built. If it had been Glasgow I wouldn't have had a second thought of driving up and of course it's further to Scotland.

As a result of this inexplicable oversight none of us fully realised the size of the three vessels until they arrived in Birkenhead on the *Gloria Sidrum* and it was only when we loaded them that we appreciated fully the stability problem we had. I must emphasise however that this was twenty-five years ago, at the time they were the largest loads ever carried on British roads, and it was really a leap into the unknown.

I will always remember with admiration the way Chief Inspector Des Southwell reacted at three minutes to six on that Sunday morning of December 5, when I told him we were not moving out from Cammell Laird's premises at Birkenhead. Bearing in mind that three footbridges had been dismantled, countless 'keep left' and other road signals removed and some thirty Mobile Police Officers were in attendance, he looked hard at me and then said, "O.K. you know best".

We then negotiated with our Dutch friends to hire in extra bogies thus allowing us to put one set of double width bogies under one end of each vessel and the job was accomplished without a hitch a fortnight later.

The largest of the three vessels measured 111ft 6ins long, with a maximum diameter of 25ft and weighted 212 tons. All three were transported in convoy from Birkenhead to the Shell Refinery at Stanlow, a distance of seventeen miles.

WYNNS personnel involved were:–

1st vessel: Driver Barry Thompson with John Dixon and Pete Collier.

2nd vessel: Driver Pete Edwards with Tom Gregory

3rd Vessel: Driver Roger Banfield with Mike Galliford

Being such an important job numerous directors and staff were also present, including H.P. Wynn, Stan Anderson, Ern Adams and Tommy Cromwell.

The Author with Chief Inspector Des Southwell, Cheshire Police.

WYNNS
SCAMMELL
CONQUEROR
NDW
836G

BERESFORD ADAMS &

WYNNS
SCAMMELL
CONQUEROR
NDW
836G

STU 27J

Probably the most important single development in connection with the movement of abnormal and indivisible loads in and around the United Kingdom was the advent of the specially designed RO/RO ship. Two such vessels were constructed for the well-known Barrow-in-Furness shipowners James Fisher and Sons Ltd, in 1966, these being the *Aberthaw Fisher* and *Kingsnorth Fisher.* Their arrival in service revolutionised the movement of heavy industrial equipment. Instead of transporting such items as transformers and stators wholly by road, it now became the norm to transport items to the nearest available suitable port to the manufacturer and ship it to the nearest port to the customer. This meant that WYNNS actually transported at both ends of the journey, and their equipment was usually on board ship for the sea journey. This method of transportation meant that larger and heavier loads could be carried.

These four photographs show sections for a cement works kiln being discharged from the vessel *Kingsnorth Fisher* at Kingsnorth Power Station prior to their road journey to the Rochester works of the Rugby Portland Cement Co. Ltd., in October, 1977.

WYNNS
Established 1963
WYNNS
WYNNS
Established in 1963

Loaded on a 14 axle trailer 5.82m wide, this 450 tonnes vessel was the largest of twenty-one carried on behalf of Blaesbjerg (UK) Ltd., at the new Mobil extension at Coryton, Essex. Measuring 37.75m long x 12m diameter the vessel was lifted off its packing on the barge using the built in hydraulics of the trailer and similarly offloaded on arrival at site. (12th March, 1979).

On the job illustrated the drivers were Roger Banfield and Syd Davies, with steersman/mates: Colin Kilby, Bill Pocock, John Jarvis, John Baulch and Mike Galliford.

WYNNS
HHB 361N
GKG 789N

WYNNS

At 1,400 tons, this module 232ft long 43ft wide and 56ft high, destined for a North Sea Oil Rig, was the heaviest load ever carried on rubber tyres. In connection with their Dutch colleagues, WYNNS moved two of these loads 500 yards at Whessoe Plant Yard, Dock Point, Middlesbrough, rolled them onto pontoons and then offloaded them using the built in hydraulic equipment in the bogies. (April, 1975).

Crew was driver Bill Wade, and on the hydraulics were John Dixon and Tom Gregory, with Stan and Eric Anderson, H.P. Wynn, Author and Rex Evans also in attendance.

Three Scammell Contractors (one brand new hence the primer paint) driven by Syd Davies, Roger Banfield and Rhydian Harries, are seen hauling a 340 tonne vessel, measuring 28.35m wide x 13.36m diameter, which was the largest of nineteen accomplished on behalf of Snamprogetti at the new extension of the Texaco Refinery, at Pembroke in 1980.

Bottom left: The outfit negotiating a 1 in 12 ascent on route to the site. The Scammells' leading are the new 640 - DBO 661V and 602 - RWO 73R.

WYNNS
SCAMMELL
SUPERIOR

WYNNS
TO LET
TYLER
DIFFUSION
Dixons
SUPERIOR
RWO 73R

WYNNS
CRYOPLANTS LTD.
POLICE
SCAMMELL

In 1977 this was the largest load ever moved through the streets of London. This Air Separation Unit measuring 98ft 11ins x 20ft 10ins x 20ft 10ins and weighing 119 tons was the largest of six boxes moved from the manufacturers Cryo Plants Ltd., Edmonton to the Royal Albert Dock, London, and then subsequently to British Oxygen, Middlesbrough.

Opposite: The load winds its way through the streets of London with RWO 73R (602) leading.

Top: The Police Motor Cycle Escort during a short break.

Above: The load arrives at the Royal Albert Dock, London.

15 9"
71000
HEAVY HAULAGE
RHA
WY

The Locomotive *71000 – the Duke of Gloucester*, weighing 85 tons was hauled on a WYNNS 7 line bogie from Barry to Quorn Railway Station for the Main Line Steam Trust. WYNNS loaded and offloaded the locomotive.

The drawing vehicle is the rebuilt and re-registered Pacific *Dreadnought* (192- NDW 345G).

Billy Pocock signals to driver Spencer David that clearance is O.K., with John Jarvis on the locomotive.

Large numbers of steam locomotives were carried all over the country mainly from the Barry premises of Woodham Bros., on behalf of individuals and firms, but mainly for Railway preservation societies, such as – the Cambrian Coast, Mid-Hants, Great Western (Didcot), Great Central, Midland, Dart Valley, West Somerset and many others.

The Author and H.P. Wynn taking delivery of the 300 ton capacity Trailer No. 999 from Cranes of Dereham on 20th March, 1966.

Gordon Wynn *(left)* and H.P. Wynn talking to Sidney Bowskill, the Birmingham Manager of Pickfords Heavy Haulage at the opening of WYNNS new depot at Chasetown on 16th September, 1976.

Ern Adams with the Author's youngest son Peter, driving a Motor tug at the Albany Street yard, obviously both are enjoying themselves.

At an Annual Dinner Dance – H.P. Wynn making a 25 year service presentation to Tommy Cromwell.

Arthur Matthews 80th Birthday Celebration on 10th August, 1979. Originally a Heavy Outfit driver, in later years he looked after the preserved Fowler Traction Engine DW 2121 .

From left (seated): Jack Blewitt, H.P. Wynn and Arthur Matthews.

(Standing): Rex Evans, Bryn Groves, Reg Blake, Tommy Cromwell, Albert Vincent, Noel Wynn and Bill Pitten.

Seen in front of Scammell JDW 147F *(from left)* Tommy Cromwell, Albert Vincent, Pete Edwards, Stan Williams and John Dixon.

These cased loads were en route from Bridgend to Liverpool Docks for export, and are seen negotiating the narrow street in Caerleon on 16th February, 1980. The height of these loads made it necessary to use many detours in order to avoid low bridges.
Above: A Scammell Amazon 100 ton 6x4 tractor unit AHB 807T (632).
Below: An Atkinson Venturer 6x4 articulated unit, XDW 578K (92).

Above: Scammell GDW 231D driven by Ian Trick heads a 54RB excavator over Caerphilly Mountain with two Diamond T tractors at the rear.

Below: Scammell Contractor TDW 83J (280) operating as an articulated low loader, laden with a Terex Dump Truck.

WYNN'S
WYNN'S
HEAVY HAULAGE
195
HEAVY HAULAGE CONTRACTORS
NEWPORT LONDON MANCHESTER
McALPINE
YDW 356

Had your GUINNESS today?
McALPINE
LOW BRIDGE
15'-6"
A 4042
A 468
A 467
HEAVY HAULAGE
RDW 976

Opposite top: Driver Rex Evans eases Pacific YDW 356 (195) and Scheuerle 8 line trailer around the Old Green Crossing, Newport, loaded with a 2400 Lima Cab from Sir Robert McAlpine's at Llanwern Steelworks en route to the new Tilbury Power Station.

Opposite bottom: Negotiating the railway bridge with the outfit's hydraulics lowered with Diamond T RDW 976 (281) as the pushing tractor. Considerable numbers of these imported excavators were received at various ports and delivered to open cast coal sites throughout the country, making it an important part of their business.

Above: An AEC 6x4 tractor unit coupled to a trailer fitted with a Scheuerle steerable bogie shown carrying a prototype Naval gun for frigates from Barrow-in-Furness to Devonport Dockyard.

WYNNS
SCAMMELL
BEDFORDIA CRANES
WYNNS
LONG VEHICLE

WYNNS
HOWARD
SCAMMELL
JDW 247F

Opposite top: Another luxury motor yacht being moved at Messrs Cushla's premises at Rochester. Pictured are the Author and wife Mo with Mr Duncan Foulds, the former Managing Director of United Transport and his wife.

Opposite bottom: Off-loading the yacht into the River Thames. Scammell JDW 247F (183) is depicted. (1973).

Above: Trailer '999' is shown rolling onto the *Kingsnorth Fisher* at South Shields with a 220 ton C.A. Parson transformer.

Above: This 337 tonne vessel measuring 124ft 10ins x 22ft 8ins x 23ft 2ins is shown approaching the offloading point at the new extension of the Texaco Refinery at Pembroke in 1980. The Scammell Contractor is DBO 661V (640)

Below: Scammell HHB 361N (196) is seen transporting an Air Product box from Ruabon, North Wales en route to Birkenhead Docks.

A Boeing 747 Freighter of Northwest Orient was used to transport an urgently required 30 tonne Electrical Rotor from Prestwick to Hong Kong, after its journey from GEC at Stafford. The use of mobile cranes to load the rotor into the high front opening of the aircraft was prohibited. Therefore, WYNNS Engineering modified a special lifting frame normally used for steel convertor changeovers, and this was used with four powered jacks to safely achieve the necessary loading height. (1979).

WYNNS
WYNNS
FDW
769E

WYNNS
WYNNS

Top left: Scammell Contractor FDW 769E (188) seen with a diesel shunting locomotive, in Birmingham.

Bottom left: One of several 120 ton gearboxes hauled from David Brown Gear Industries, Huddersfield, to Manchester for shipment by RO/RO vessel to Vickers, Barrow-in-Furness, and Swan Hunter at Hartlepool. These were for installation in through-deck cruisers.

Above: A convoy of five Scammell Contractors with wide cases en route to Cardiff Docks for export are seen on the M4 Motorway at Highcross, near Newport, before this section was widened to three lane.

Overleaf: A Submarine section weighing 550 tons is moved within the shipyard at Barrow-in-Furness on a 17 line Nicholas trailer in 1979.

WYNNS
WYNNS
Established 1863
633
Contractor
SCAMMELL
MUSKETEER

When I decided on the name of this second book I had no idea that by the time it was ready for publishing I would be able to proudly announce the formation of a new company called WYNNS LTD.

My youngest son Peter is responsible for this new venture and it goes without saying that everyone who remembers the 'old' WYNNS wish him every success.

He can be reached on: Tel. 01785 850411
Fax. 01785 851866

Work has commenced on a third WYNNS book devoted to the activities of the firm overseas. I intend to continue work towards other volumes, and to that end would welcome hearing from anyone who can assist.

Please contact me at
7, Quebec Close,
Glasllwych
Newport
Gwent, NP9 3RA
Tel. 01633 251388